Umrah All You Need to Know

By

Dr. Farah Alam-Mirza

Contents

Part One - Ziyarahs in Makkah

Part Two- Ziyarahs in Madinah

Section Three- Duas and Prayers

Introduction

This book is a complete guide to Umrah and Ziyarah. In Section One you will learn how to prepare for Umrah, the rituals in performing Umrah, with details of duas to be recited at specific points. There is some mention of Hadiths to aid understanding.

Section Two is about the Ziyarahs or places to visit in Makkah and Madinah. There is some detail of the historical significance of the locations and duas to be recited there.

Section Three contains some prayers, daroods and duas that can be recited during Tawaf and Sa'iy. They are not compulsory, but are just a reminder for you.

How to use this book

If you are performing Umrah for the first time, then this book will be helpful for you. Try to read it before you go so you can understand what is required beforehand. This book is a detailed guide on Umrah with photos of locations to aid understanding.

The other book in this series "Umrah Made Easy," is a much shorter concise book with to the point information on the rituals of Umrah, that can be carried around easily and read at the time of performing Umrah.

Section One- Umrah

What is Umrah?

The word Umrah comes from I'tamara which means "to intend to visit." Umrah or the minor pilgrimage is an act of worship with the intention to visit the House of Allah, the Kaaba in Makkah. It is a Sunnah of the Prophet, sallalahu alaihi wassallam (SAW) or peace be upon him (SAW). The Prophet (SAW) performed four umrahs in his life. It can be performed anytime during the year except in the 5-days of Hajj from 9th to 13th Dhul-Hijjah.

Blessings of Umrah

Umrah increases the acceptance of dua. Any travel increases the acceptance of dua, but travel to the House of Allah increases the blessings of dua even more. Pilgrims are the guests of Allah; he called them and they answered, therefore if they ask, they will be given. Pilgrims have the added benefit of their positive state; they are in the state of Ihraam. Umrah removes poverty and increases wealth.

Hadith
Regarding the benefits, virtues and excellence of Umrah,
The Prophet (SAW) said:
- "An Umrah during Ramadan is equivalent to Hajj," (Bukhari, Muslim).
- "One Umrah is expiation for the sins committed between it and the next Umrah, if the major sins are avoided." (Bukhari, Muslim).
- "Perform Hajj and Umrah again and again for both remove poverty and sins, like a furnace purifies gold and silver and iron." (Tirmidhi).
- "The jihad of the old and weak and women is Hajj and Umrah."(Tirmidhi).

Steps of Umrah:

1. Ihraam: special dressing at Meeqat
2. Niyyah: intention
3. Talbiyah: verbalisation of intention
4. Tawaf: around the Kaaba seven times
5. Multazim: two rakaat salah at Muqaam-e-Ibrahim
6. Sa'iy: seven circuits between Safa and Marwa
7. Halaq: shaving or cutting hair, removal of Ihraam

Fiqh of Umrah:
Fiqh is the theoretical basis of the teachings of the Quran and Sunnah.

Arkaan of Umrah:
 Arkaan is the plural of 'rukn,' which means an essential pillar of any ritual. There are three arkaans of Umrah:
1. Ihraam
2. Tawaf
3. Sai'y

Waajibat
A waajib is an obligatory act of a ritual. The difference between rukn and waajib is if you miss a waajib you have to do a **kaffara** which means expiation by means of sacrificing an animal, feeding six poor people or fasting for three days.

 There are two waajibat; at the beginning and one at the end of Umrah. They are:
1. To enter into Ihraam after passing the meeqat. If you pass the meeqat without Ihraam, you will need to go back and make Ihraam, or continue and make Ihraam and give sacrifice.
2. Shave or trim the hair.
Everything else is Sunnah.

Meeqat

Meeqats are specific locations that the Prophet (SAW) assigned on all four sides of Makkah, where one intending to perform Hajj or Umrah must enter the state of Ihraam. The pilgrim must not pass through the Meeqat without assuming Ihraam.

The Meeqats designated by the Prophet (SAW) are as follows:

 1. Dhul-Hulayfah: also known as Abyar Ali is the meeqat for people coming from Medina. It is about 450 km away.

 2. Al- Juhfah: also known as Rabigh, is the meeqat for pilgrims coming from Egypt and Syria. It is about 187 km northwest of Makkah.

3. Dhat-ul Irq: is the meeqat for pilgrims coming from Iran and Iraq. it is about 94 km northeast of Makkah.

4. Qarn-al-Manazil: is the meeqat for pilgrims coming from Najd and Taif and the Gulf States. It is also known as As- Sayl-al Kabeer. It is about 94 km east of Makkah.

5. Yalumlum: is the meeqat for pilgrims coming from India, Pakistan, Yemen and the south. It is about 54 km southwest of Makkah.

Pilgrims arriving by air

 Pilgrims travelling by plane should perform ghusl before boarding the plane and wear the Ihraam before the meeqat. Saudi airlines announce the meeqat, which is about an hour before reaching Jeddah airport. Not all airlines announce the meeqat. It is better to wear the Ihraam beforehand, because if you miss it then you will have to go back to the nearest meeqat again before you can perform Umrah.

Masjid-e-Ayesha is the meeqat for people staying in Makkah. (See section on Ziyarahs for more details).

1. Ihraam

Ihraam is the state that the pilgrim enters with the intention to make Hajj or Umrah. From the Fiqh perspective, Ihraam is the declaration that you are performing Umrah. Ihraam is a rukn to do before the tawaf begins and it is waajib to do at the meeqat.

How to enter into Ihraam

Cut your nails, remove unwanted hair and perform ghusl (bath) or wudoo. Performing ghusl is a Sunnah. Men are to wear the clothes of Ihraam, preferably of white colour, consisting of two sheets of unstitched cloth to cover the lower part of the body and one for the upper half. The head must be left uncovered. A pair of simple sandals leaving the ankle bones bare can be worn. Women's ordinary clothes are their Ihraam, as long as the whole body is covered except for the face.

Reasons for wearing Ihraam

 1. To make the person humble, as rich and poor all are dressed alike.
 2. As a show of unity, as the Muslims become one as they perform Umrah.
 3. As a reminder of the shroud that we will wear when we depart this world.

Prohibitions of Ihraam
1. Cutting or shaving hair: combing is allowed. Shedding hair does not affect Ihraam.
2. Trimming nails.
3. Applying perfume or anything fragrant.
4. Hunting animals.
5. Wearing stitched clothes- for men only.
6. Wearing a garment over the head- for men.
7. Ladies must not wear gloves or niqab ie covering their face.
8. Khitbah or making a marriage proposal.
9. Sexual intimacy or speech or suggestion of it.
10. Conflict, transgression, verbal or physical harm to anyone.

The Prophet (SAW) used to perform 2 raka'at nafil with the intention of Ihraam. In the first raka'at it is Sunnah to recite Surah Kafiroon, and in the second raka'at recite Surah Ikhlas.

2. Niyyah or intention

Make Niyyah at the meeqat and recite this dua:

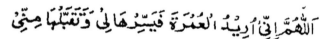

Allaahumma innee ureedul umrata fayassirhaa lee wataqabbalhaa minnee.

Translation: "Oh Allah I intend to perform Umrah, make it easy for me and accept it from me."

3. Talbiyah

Talbiyah is a prayer invoked by the pilgrim that they intend to perform Umrah or Hajj, only for the glory of Allah. Upon assuming Ihraam at the meeqat the pilgrim should begin calling out the

Talbiyah. Men should recite it in an audible voice intermittently throughout, while ladies should say it in a low voice.

The dua for Talbiyah is:

$$لَبَّيْكَ اَللّٰهُمَّ لَبَّيْكَ ۔ لَبَّيْكَ لَا شَرِيْكَ لَكَ لَبَّيْكَ$$
$$اِنَّ الْحَمْدَ وَالنِّعْمَةَ لَكَ وَالْمُلْكَ لَا شَرِيْكَ لَكَ$$

Labbayk allaahumma labbayk.
Labbayka laa sharika laka labbayk.
Innal hamda wanni' mata laka wal mulk laa sharika lak.

Translation: "Here I am here Oh Allah, here I am, there is no partner for You, here I am. Truly all praise and favour is Yours, and Sovereignty. You have no partner."

Keep reciting the Talbiyah until you see the Kaaba. Make dua, istighfar and refrain yourselves from worldly concerns. The Ihraam becomes complete on making Niyyah and reciting the Talbiyah.

Entering the Masjid al-Haram:

Enter the sacred city of Makkah Mukarramah with utmost respect and humility. Make arrangements to go to the Masjid al-Haram immediately. It is Sunnah to enter the mosque with your right foot first saying the following dua:

$$بِسْمِ اللهِ وَالصَّلٰوةُ وَالسَّلَامُ عَلٰى رَسُوْلِ اللهِ$$
$$اَللّٰهُمَّ افْتَحْ لِى اَبْوَابَ رَحْمَتِكَ$$

Bismillaahi wassaaltu was salamu alaa rasoolillaah.
Allaahummaftah lee abwaaba rahmatik.

Translation: "In the name of Allah, peace and blessings be upon the Messenger of Allah. Oh Allah, open for me the doors of your mercy."

Upon seeing the Kaaba say three times:

Allahu akbar. Laa ilaaha illallaah.

Translation: "Allah is the greatest. There is no God except Allah."

Then recite the Darood Sharif and make dua as much as you can, as whatever dua made with good intention at this time is most certainly accepted by Allah if it is in your favour.

4. Tawaf

Tawaf is the act of walking round the Kaaba seven times in the counter- clockwise direction while reciting duas. Tawaf is fard in umrah.

Men should keep the right arm and shoulder bare and cover the left shoulder with their Ihraam. This is called **"Idhtiba."** You need to be in the state of purity and wudu while performing tawaf.

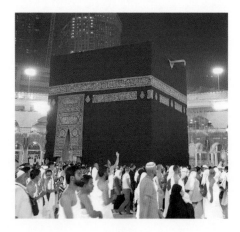

Hadith: The Prophet (SAW) said: "Tawaf is a prayer similar to salah, except that you may speak during it. So when you do tawaf, do not speak anything but what is good (Tirmidhi).

"Tawaf is prayer, so when you do tawaf, speak little." (Ahmad).

Start the tawaf from the corner of the Kaaba where the **Black Stone** is, (**Hajra Aswad**). You will see a green light directly opposite the corner of the Kaaba where the Hajra Aswad is, this is where you start and end the seven tawafs.

Hajra Aswad or Black Stone

The Hajra Aswad or Black Stone is set in the eastern corner of the Kaaba. The Hajra Aswad was brought from Jannah by Jibrael Alaihissalam (AS) and given to Prophet Ibrahim (AS) to be placed in the corner of the Kaaba when he was originally building the Kaaba.

Hadith: Ibn Abbas razi alla anhu (RA) or may Allah be pleased with him narrated that the Prophet (SAW) said the Black Stone came down from Paradise and it was whiter than milk, but the sins of the sons of Adam turned it Black (Tirmidhi).

Duas are accepted at the Hajra Aswad, and on the Day of Judgement it will testify in favour of all those who kissed it. The

Prophet (SAW) said "By Allah! On the the day of qiyamah Allah will present the Hajra Aswad in a way that it will have two eyes and a tongue to testify to the imaan (faith) of all those who kissed it." (Tirmidhi).

Performing Tawaf

Start from the Hajra Aswad or be in line with it. No particular dua or supplication was prescribed by the Prophet for tawaf. Just stay spiritual and connect with Allah. The pilgrim may recite any dua or supplication of their choice; see the Duas section for some reminders and examples. It is better to offer any supplication that you remember by heart as reading can be difficult due to the crowds.

If possible, touch the Black Stone with your hand, kiss it and place your forehead on it. If this is not possible, then just point towards it with your right hand. This is known as **"Istilam"**. Recite this dua:

$$\text{بِسْمِ اللهِ اَللّٰهُ اَكْبَرُ}$$

Bismillahi allaahu akbar

Translation: "In the name of Allah, Allah is the Greatest."

This is to be done at the beginning and end of each round of the tawaf. Walk round the Kaaba, with the Kaaba on your left. Each time you reach the Black Stone to begin your next Tawaf, repeat the above action and dua, till seven circuits are complete. Men are to walk fast, if possible, for the first three tawafs, this is called **"Ramal."**

Hadith: The Prophet (SAW) said: "No man lifts his foot and sets it down but ten good deeds are recorded for him, and ten bad deeds are erased from his record, and he will be raised thereby ten degrees in status."(Tirmidhi).

Rukn-al-Yamani or the Yemeni corner

This is the corner of the Kaaba before the Black Stone. It is Sunnah to touch it with the right hand if possible.

Hadith: The Prophet (SAW) said, "Touching the Hajra Aswad and Rukn Yamani erases sins." (Tirmidhi).

Recite the following dua between the Yemeni corner and the Black Stone:

رَبَّنَا اٰتِنَا فِى الـدُّنْيَا حَسَنَةً وَّفِى الْاٰخِرَةِ حَسَنَةً وَّقِنَا عَذَابَ النَّارِ

Rabbana aatina fid duniya hasanatan wa fil aakhirati hasanatan wa qinaa azaban nar.

Translation: "Our Lord, give us in this world that which is good and in the hereafter that which is good and protect us from the punishment of the fire."

5. Multazim, Maqaam-e-Ibrahim: Station of Ibrahim

The Muqaam-e-Ibrahim refers to the location of the stone on which Prophet Ibrahim (AS) stood on while he was building the Kaaba. Allah made the trace of his footprints to remain on the stone as a reminder for believers.

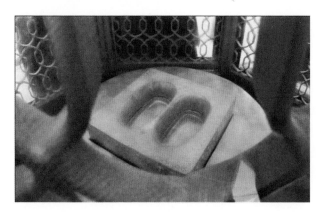

Hadith: It is reported from Saeed bin Jubair (may Allah be pleased with him) that the Prophet (SAW) said: "The stone is the Station of Ibrahim. Allah made it soft and made it a mercy. Ibrahim AS would stand on it and Ismail AS would hand stones up to him."(Muthir-al-Gharami).

Allah revealed in the verse in the Quran in Surah Baqarah:

"Take the station of Ibrahim as a place of prayer (Salah)," 2:125.

Men should cover their shoulders with their Ihraam now. After completing the tawaf proceed towards the Station of Ibrahim and recite this dua:

وَٱتَّخِذُوا۟ مِن مَّقَامِ إِبْرَٰهِۦمَ مُصَلًّى

Wattakhizu mim maqam-e Ibrahima musalla

Translation: "And take the station of Ibrahim as a place of prayer."

Pray two raka'ats behind Muqaam-e- Ibrahim. It is sunnah to recite Surah Kafiroon (Qul yaa ayyuhal kaafiroon) in the first raka'at, and Surah Ikhlas (Qul huwallaahu ahad) in the second. If there's a lot of crowd at the Muqaam-e-Ibrahim, then it is fine to pray the two raka'ats anywhere within the Masjid al-Haram where possible.

Hadith: The Prophet (SAW) said: "Whoever performs seven tawafs and then prays two raka'ats it will be equal to him freeing a believing slave."(Tirmidhi).

Drinking Zamzam

Next proceed towards the arched walls of the mosque behind the Muqaam-e- Ibrahim and drink Zamzam water. It is Sunnah to make dua after drinking Zamzam water and pour some over your head. The fountain of Zamzam is located within the Masjid al-Haram. It is the heritage of Prophet Ismail (AS) and his mother Hajara (AS). It contains both blessings and health. There are many water coolers with Zamzam water freely available inside the Haram.

Hadith: The Prophet (SAW) said "Zamzam water is for whatever intention one drinks it." (Saheeh).
"It satisfies as food and cures illness." (Saheeh).

Abdullah bin Mubarak said, "I drink this water to quench the thirst of the day of judgement."
Abdullah bin Abbas said, "Oh Allah I ask for beneficial knowledge, abundant provision and healing from all desires."

It is sunnah to go back to **Multazim** and make dua. Multazim is at the area between the Hajra Aswad and the door of the Kaaba.

6. Sa'iy

Sa'iy is the act of walking between the two small hills of Safa and Marwa seven times. Follow the signs to Masa'al Safa.

Sa'iy commemorates the actions of Hajara (AS) the wife of Prophet Ibrahim (AS) who walked between the hills of Safa and Marwa seven times in search of water for her baby son Ismael. In her desperation she climbed the hills to get a better view of the area to get help. In between the hills she ran. The angel Jibrael (AS) hit the ground with his wing, and a stream of water gushed forth, which is the location of the fountain of Zamzam.

Upon approaching the foot of Safa, recite the following dua:

$$إِنَّ ٱلصَّفَا وَٱلْمَرْوَةَ مِن شَعَآئِرِ ٱللَّهِ$$

$$فَمَنْ حَجَّ ٱلْبَيْتَ أَوِ ٱعْتَمَرَ فَلَا جُنَاحَ عَلَيْهِ أَن يَطَّوَّفَ$$

$$بِهِمَا ۚ وَمَن تَطَوَّعَ خَيْرًا فَإِنَّ ٱللَّهَ شَاكِرٌ عَلِيمٌ$$

Innas safa wal marwata min sha'aa-i-rillah. Faman hajjal baita awi'tamara fala junaha alaihi an yatawwafa bihimaa. Wa man tatawwa'a khayran fa innallaha shakirun 'aleem.

Translation: "Verily Safa and Marwa are from the symbols of Allah. So, it is not a sin on him who performs Hajj or Umrah of the House of Kaaba to compass them round. And whoever does good voluntarily, then verily, Allah is the All- Recogniser the All- Knower."

The Prophet (SAW) also recited:

$$نَبْدَأُ بِمَا بَدَأَ اللَّهُ بِهِ$$

Nabda'u bima bada Allahu bihi.

"We begin with what Allah began with."

Then climb onto Safa and recite the following dua three times while facing the Kaaba.

$$اللهُ أَكْبَرُ، اللهُ أَكْبَرُ، اللهُ أَكْبَرُ.$$

$$لَا إِلَهَ إِلاَّ اللَّهُ وَحْدَهُ لَاشَرِيكَ لَهُ ، لَهُ الْمُلْكُ وَلَهُ الْحَمْدُ وَهُوَ عَلَى$$

$$كُلِّ شَيْءٍ قَدِيرٌ ، لاَ إِلَهَ إِلاَّ اللَّهُ وَحْدَهُ أَنْجَزَ وَعْدَهُ ، وَنَصَرَ عَبْدَهُ$$

$$وَهَزَمَ الأَحْزَابَ وَحْدَهُ.$$

Allahu akbar, Allahu akbar, Allahu akbar, Laa ilaha illallahu wahdahu la sharika lahu, lahul mulku wala hul hamdu, wa huwa'alaa qulli shay in qadeer. Laa ilaha illallahu wahdahu, anjaza wa'dahu wa nasara 'abdahu wa hazamal ahzaba wahdahu.

Translation: "Allah is the Greatest, Allah is the Greatest, Allah is the Greatest. None has the right to be worshipped except Allah alone, who has no partner. To Him belongs the Dominion, to Him belongs all praise, and He has power over everything. He fulfilled His promise, gave victory to His servant, and defeated the confederates alone."

The Prophet (SAW) would face the Kaaba and make long dua here. Recite the Darood Sharif and remain engaged in dua, as this is a place when duas are accepted.

Then descend towards Marwa, remain engaged in prayer and supplications, there are no particular supplications to be recited between Safa and Marwa. For a list of suggestions see the section on duas.

Above you will see some fluorescent green lights for a part of the distance between Safa and Marwa. Quicken your pace and run slowly if possible, for the duration of the green lights, this is called **"Ramal."** Ladies can walk normally. This is where Hajara (AS) would run while in the valley so she could keep a physical eye on her child. Remember the spirituality, tawakkul, iman and patience of Prophet Ibrahim (AS) and Hajara (AS) while performing Sa'iy.

After the green lights resume your normal pace till you reach Marwa. Safa to Marwa is one round.

Once you ascend Marwa repeat the dua made before when ascending Safa. At Marwa face in the direction of Kaaba and make Dua. Then complete seven rounds, the last one ending at Marwa.

7. Halaq or shaving hair

After completing Sa'iy, men must shave their head or trim the hair from all over the head, shaving is more virtuous. Ladies should shorten their hair by a fingertip's length from the end of their hair.

Hadith: The Prophet (SAW) said: "Shaving has three times the thawab of trimming." The Prophet prayed for those who shaved their head three times, and for those who cut their hair once. (Al-Mawsoo'ah al fiqhiyyah).

After cutting the hair or Halaq, the rituals of Umrah are completed and the state of Ihraam has ended.

Congratulations on completing your Umrah! May Allah accept your Umrah and bestow you with all its blessings.

Section 2- Ziyarahs

What is Ziyarah?

Ziyarah means "to visit."The holy cities of Makkah and Madinah are full of history. Visiting the important landmarks will help you gain more awareness on the history and significance of these places.

Part One: Ziyarahs in Makkah

Mount Thawr (Saur): Jabal-Al-Thawr

Is a mountain in Makkah which has the cave in which the Prophet (SAW) and Abu Bakr (RA) sought refuge from the Quraish for three days and nights as they were migrating from Makkah to Madinah.

While they were inside the cave, Allah sent a spider that spun a web across the entrance of the cave. Two doves came and made a nest between the spider's web and a tree at the cave and laid eggs. When the Quraish came looking for the men, they wanted to search inside the cave but when they saw the spider's web and dove's nest outside they left, as they thought no one could have entered the cave, and so the Prophet and Abu Bakr remained safe in Mount Thawr.

Mount Hira or Jabal- Al Hira or Jabal- e Noor, the Mountain of Light, Ghar-e-Hira or the Cave of Hira

Jabal- Hira is about 2 km from the Kaaba. At the top of the mountain is the cave where the Prophet (SAW) received the first revelation of the Holy Quran. The Prophet (SAW) would spend hours in the cave meditating in solitude.

In the month of Ramadan in 610 CE the angel Jibrael (AS) (Gabriel) came to the Prophet (SAW) with the first revelation of the Quran.

Masjid-e-Jinn

Masjid-e-Jinn is a mosque in Makkah where hundreds of Jinn came to listen to the Prophet (SAW) reciting the Quran, and they all accepted Islam there.

Jabal-e Rahmat, Mountain of Mercy or Mount Arafat

Jabal-Rahmat is a hill in Makkah in Arafat. It is the location where the Prophet Adam (AS) and his wife Hawwa (AS) met after being cast down to Earth from heaven, after they ate the forbidden fruit. There is a monument there to mark the place where they met.

Monument on Jabal-e Rahmat

People pray salah and make dua to Allah here.

Masjid-e Nimrah

This mosque is situated in Arafat. The Prophet delivered his famous farewell sermon there, shortly before his death. Every year on the 9th of Dhul Hajj a sermon is delivered, and Zuhr and Asr prayers are offered by pilgrims for Hajj.

Masjid-e Ayesha or Masjid-e Taneem

Masjid-e- Ayesha is a mosque in Makkah about 5 miles away from the Kaaba. It is the place where the Prophet's wife Ayesha (RA) went to enter Ihraam for Umrah, on the instruction of the Prophet (SAW). It is a Meeqat for Umrah for people staying in Makkah.

Arafat

The plains of Arafat lie between the hills of Arafat. This is where the Prophet Adam (AS) was reunited with his wife Hawwah (AS). All pilgrims have to stay at Arafat at the time of Hajj on 9 th Dhul Hajj. Arafat is the best place to make Dua, as duas are accepted here. Arafat is the location where all people will be gathered on the Day of Judgement.

Minah

Minah is a valley in the east of Makkah. It is known as the "Tent City," as during Hajj, pilgrims stay in Minah in tents. More than 100,000 air-conditioned tents provide temporary accommodation for the pilgrims performing Hajj.

Jamarat

The Jamarat are three stone pillars located in the valley of Minah. The stones represent the locations where Shaytan tried to dissuade Prophet Ibrahim (AS) when he was taking his son Ismael for sacrifice. The Jamarat are pelted with stones by the pilgrims during Hajj.

The three pillars are called Jamarat-al-Ula, Jamarat-al-Wusta and Jamarat-al-Aqaba.

Prophet Ibrahim (AS) saw a dream for three nights that he was sacrificing his son Ismael. He knew this was a revelation from Allah. He took his young son and on the way he told him about his dream. Ismail readily agreed and told his father to cover his face so he would not falter. On the way he was met by Shaytan (the devil) at three locations, where he tried to dissuade Prophet Ibrahim (AS). The angel Jibrael (AS) said to pelt Shaytan with stones. The Jamarat symbolise these locations. There is a bridge connecting the Jamarat to make it easy for pilgrims to access them during Hajj.

Muzdalifah

Muzdalifah is a flat region of open space between Arafat and Minah. It is about four kilometers long. During Hajj, pilgrims perform Maghrib and Isha salah together here, and stay the night here without any proper bed under the open sky, and leave before sunrise. Pilgrims collect pebbles here for stoning at the Jamarat.

Wadi-e- Muhassar

Wadi-e-Muhassar is a valley located between Minah and Muzadlifah. It is famous as it is the place where Allah destroyed Abraha and his army of elephants. The story is mentioned in the Quran in Surah Feel.

Abraha-al-Ashram was the Governor of Yemen. He wanted to take the Kaaba, demolish it and set up a place of worship. In the year 571 CE he set out for Makkah with his army on elephants. When the army reached Wadi-e-Muhassar, Allah sent down little birds called Aba-beel, with pebbles in their mouths. They pelted the army with their stones destroying them all. That is how Allah saved the Kaaba.

Wadi-e-Muhassar (Islamic Guardian 2018).

After this incident Arabs visited the Kaaba from all parts of the region. It was called the "Year of the Elephant." The Prophet (SAW) was born soon after this event. During Hajj it is Sunnah to pass through this region briskly as it was the place of punishment from Allah.

Jannat-ul- Muallah

Jannat-ul-Muallah is a famous cemetery located in Makkah. It is famous for the historical people buried here, such as Khadija (RA), the wife of the Prophet, Abd Manaf, the great- great grandfather of the Prophet. Hashim the great-grandfather of the Prophet, Abdul Mutallib grandfather of the Prophet, Abu Talib uncle of the Prophet.

It is Sunnah to say salaam to the dead when passing by a graveyard. It is in **hadith** that the dead respond to the salaam of a believer.

Dua for visiting Graveyards

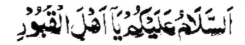

Translation: Peace be onto you Oh people of the graves.

Cemetery from the time of Jahiliyah

This is a small area to the south west of the Haram, where pagan Arabs used to bury their newborn baby girls alive. This was before the advent of Islam, when the Arabs believed that daughters were a sign of disgrace. The Prophet (SAW) put an end to such practices.

Part Two: Ziyarahs in Madinah

While en route or in Madinah Munawwarah, recite the Darood Sharif (salutations upon the Prophet) as much as possible. Enter Madinah with humility and humbleness. This is the city of our beloved Prophet (SAW), this is where he lived and died. He is buried in the Masjid-e- Nabawi. Try and follow Sunnah as much as possible.

Masjid-e-Nabawi

The Masjid-e-Nabawi or the Prophet's Mosque was built by the Prophet Mohammad (SAW) after he settled in Madinah on emigration (Hijra) from Makkah in 622 CE.

It was originally built adjacent to his house. Subsequently it underwent great expansion and today it is the second largest mosque in the world after the Masjid-al Haram in Makkah. It has very beautiful architecture and structure.

Enter the mosque with your right foot and recite the dua for entering any mosque.

بِسْمِ اللهِ وَالصَّلٰوةُ وَالسَّلَامُ عَلٰى رَسُوْلِ اللهِ
اَللّٰهُمَّ افْتَحْ لِيْ اَبْوَابَ رَحْمَتِكَ

Bismillahi wassalatu wassalaamu ala rasulillah, allahummaftah li abwaba rahmatik.

Translation: "In the name of Allah blessings and peace be upon the Messenger of Allah. Oh Allah, open to me the doors of your mercy." (Al-Bukhari, Muslim and others).

Hadith:
Abu Hurairah (RA) narrated that the Prophet (SAW) said: "A prayer in my masjid is better than a thousand offered in any other, except for Masjid-al Haram," (Bukhari).

The Prophet (SAW) said, "He who performs forty salah in my Masjid and does not miss a single salah, Allah prescribes for him freedom from the fire, freedom from punishment and freedom from hypocrisy." -Musnad Al Imam Ahmad.

Rawdah Mubarak

The Prophet's grave is located in the Masjid-e- Nabawi, in the Green Dome. He was buried in the house of Ayesha (RA). It is called the Rawdah Mubarak. Outside the grave is a gold mesh enclosure.

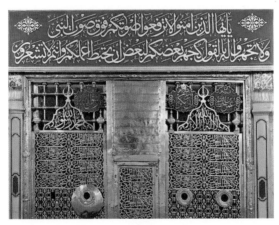

Hadith:
There are many Hadiths on visiting the Prophet's Rawdah.

-The Prophet (SAW) said: "Whoever visits my grave, my intercession will be obligatory for him." (Ibn Khuzaymah, Al-Bazzar).
-Abdullah Ibn Umar reported that the Prophet said: "Whoever visits me, and has no other motive, has a right over me that I intercede on his behalf on the Day of Judgement." (Al-Tabrani and Taqi-ad-Din).
-"Whoever visits my grave is as if he visited me during my life."(Al-Tabrani).

Visiting the Prophet's grave:

Keep reciting the Darood Sharif. The Prophet (SAW) was buried with his two companions, the Rashidun Caliphs: Abu Bakr (RA) and Umar (RA) on either side. At the grave of the Prophet recite salam salutation as:

اَلصَّلوٰةُ وَالسَّلَامُ عَلَيْكَ يَا رَسُوْلَ اللهِ ﻬ

"Assalatu wassalamu alayka ya rasulallah."
"Peace and salutations be upon you, O Messenger of Allah."

At the grave of Abu Bakr (RA) say salaam as:

السَّلامُ عَلَيْكَ يَاأَبَا بَكْر

"Peace be upon you O, Abu Bakr,"

And near the grave of Umar (RA) say,

السَّلامُ عَلَيْكَ يَاعُمَر

"Peace be upon you O, Umar."

After salam, make dua to Allah through the wasilah (medium) of the Prophet (SAW), asking Allah to forgive you and to grant your wishes through the blessings of the Prophet. Ask for the shafa'at (intercession) of the Prophet (SAW) on your behalf. Remember dua is made to Allah only.

"Verily Allah and his angels bless the Prophet, Oh you who believe send your blessings on him and greet him with a salutation worthy of the respect (due to him)." Surah 33, Ayat 56.

Riyadul- Jannah

Inside the Prophet's mosque, there is a place between the holy grave and the Prophet's mimbar* or pulpit, about which he said:

Hadith: "Between my house and my mimbar lies a garden from the gardens of Paradise." (Bukhari and Muslim).

Try to pray two raka'ats at the Rawdah as the Prophet (SAW) distinguished it for being a garden from the gardens of Paradise. It is distinguished by a green carpet; the rest of the mosque has a red carpet. Make dua here.

* The mimbar is a pulpit in the mosque where the Imam (prayer leader) stands to deliver sermons.

Masjid Quba
During the migration from Makkah to Madinah, the Prophet (SAW) along with Abu Bakr (RA) stayed at a village called Quba on the outskirts of Madinah. This migration marks the beginning of the Islamic calendar or Hijra on 12th of Rabi-ul-Awwal, 16th July 622 CE.
The people of Quba give a warm welcome to the Prophet (SAW). He stayed there for several days and laid the foundations of Masjid Quba.

This is the first mosque to be built in Islam. The Prophet (SAW) helped build Quba Mosque and prayed there. Then he continued his journey to the city of Yathrib which was later named Madinah Munawwarah. Outside the mosque is a plaque which says the following:

Almighty God says:

"There is a mosque whose foundation was laid from the first date on piety; it is more worthy of the standing forth (for prayer) therein. In it are men who love to be purified, and Allah loves those who purify themselves. (Al Tawba 9:108).

The Prophet (SAW) used to visit Quba mosque every Saturday, sometimes riding and sometimes on foot to offer there two raka'ats. (Bukhari).

The Prophet (SAW) is reported to have said: "Whoever goes out to offer prayers in this Mosque Quba, will have the reward of performing an umrah."

Masjid Qiblatain or Mosque of the two Qiblas

This mosque is of great historic importance, as in 2 AH, the revelation came to the Prophet (SAW) while he was praying in this mosque, to change the direction of prayer from the Bait-al-Muqaddis in Jerusalem to the Kaaba in Makkah.

When the Prophet (SAW) was in Makkah, he prayed towards the Bait-al- Muqaddis with the Kaaba in front of him. He hoped it would be changed to the Kaaba. While he was praying afternoon salah in Masjid Qiblatain, he received the revelation (wahi) to change his direction of prayer towards the Kaaba.

"Verily we have seen your face turned towards the heavens, so we will turn you to a Qibla (prayer direction) that will please you. So turn your face towards the sacred mosque (Masjid al-Haram), and wherever you may be turn your face towards it. (2:144).

The Prophet (SAW) turned towards the Kaaba and completed his prayers. From that day onwards, the Kaaba became the new Qibla for muslims. The muslims rejoiced at the change of the Qibla but the Jews were unhappy. A prophecy in the Jews' ancient books had been fulfilled that the last Prophet would change the direction of prayer from Jerusalem to the house of Ibrahim. They approached the Prophet (SAW) and asked if he would revert the orientation back to Jerusalem, then they would follow him.

Allah revealed in Surah Baqarah (2.145), "Even if you were to bring to those who were given the Book every proof, they would not follow your direction, nor are you to follow their direction."

Jannat-ul-Baqi (Garden of Heaven)

Jannat-ul-Baqi is the oldest cemetery of Islam in Madinah. Several members of the Prophet's close family are buried here, along with ten thousand of his companions (Sahaba). The wives of the Prophet (SAW), Ayesha, Sauda, Hafsa, Zainab, Jawairiya, Umme Habiba, Safiya, Zainab, Umme Salma are buried here. The daughters of the Prophet (SAW), Fatima, Zainab and Umme Kulsoom are buried here. The Prophet's uncle Abbas and his grandson Hassan and great-grandson Zainul Abideen and other descendants are also buried here.

Usman (RA) the third Caliph and son-in-law of the Prophet (SAW) is buried here too. Halima Sadia, the wet nurse of the Prophet (SAW) is buried here. Make dua for all those buried in Jannat-ul-Baqi.

Mount Uhud: Jabal-e- Uhud

Jabal-e-Uhud is a mountain in Madinah where the second battle in Islam, the Battle of Uhud was fought in 3 AH.

Hadith: The Prophet (SAW) said, "Uhud is a mountain that loves us, and we love it." (Muslim).

A year earlier in 2 AH at the Battle of Badr, the Quraish of Makkah suffered a humiliating defeat by the Muslims. After their defeat, the Quraish formed a large army of three to five thousand men led by Abu Sufiyan to attack the Muslims in Madinah to avenge their dead. Hind was the daughter of Utbah and Abu Sufiyan's wife. Khalid bin Waleed, Ikrimah Ibn Abi Jahl and Amar Ibn-al- As were in their army. These three later converted to Islam and became famous generals. The Prophet (SAW) left Madinah

for the valley of Mount Uhud with a small army of only seven
hundred men. Fifty arches were instructed by the Prophet (SAW)
to position themselves on a hill opposite, so that the Muslims had
cover from that side. They were instructed to stay there and to
obstruct the enemy if they attacked the Muslims from the rear.

Shuhuda Uhud Mosque

A fierce battle ensued and the Muslims were hopeful for victory,
the Quraish were retreating. At that point the archers left their
position and came onto the battlefield to collect the spoils of war.
Just then, a group of the Quraish lead by Khalid bin Waleed on
horseback took advantage and attacked the Muslims from the
back side. The Muslims suffered a huge loss and about seventy
of the Prophet's closest companions were martyred, including his
uncle Hamza, his cousin Abdullah Ibn Jahsh, and the flag bearer,
Musab Ibn Omair. In this battle, the Prophet (SAW) was injured
and his tooth was broken.

Hind, the wife of Abu Sufiyan took revenge by mutilating the body
of the Prophet's uncle, Hamza (RA). When the Prophet (SAW)
saw his uncle's mutilated body, he was overcome with emotion.
The angel Jibrael (AS) informed him that the name of Hamza had

been written in the seven heavens as "Hamza Ibn Abdul Muttalib: Lion of Allah and Lion of his Messenger."

"And do not say about those are killed in the way of Allah, 'Dead,' they are alive but you know not." (Baqarah 2:154).

Shuhudah Uhud Graveyard

The graves of the seventy martyrs of Uhud are near the mountain in an enclosure titled, **"Shuhudah."** You can pay them a visit and recite Fatiha there.

Khandaq and Seven Mosques

In the fifth year of Hijra, the polytheists along with the Jews formed a coalition and waged another battle against the Muslims. Salman Al- Farsi (RA), a close companion of the Prophet (SAW), suggested digging a trench around Madinah to stop the advance of the enemies, hence the battle is called the Battle of the Trench or Khandaq. Seven mosques were built during the Battle of Khandaq.

The Muslim army camped at the foothill of the Mount Sala, facing the trench. The coalition of the Quraish led by Amr Ibn Abd Wudd, who was said to be equal to a thousand soldiers, managed to pass over the trench, and challenged the Muslims. He was killed by Ali Ibn Abi Talib (RA), the Prophet's cousin and son-in-law, who was sent by the Prophet (SAW) to fight Amr.

Strong winds began to batter the coalition camp, and they retreated in a state of panic and confusion. The Muslims were outnumbered by the enemy but due to the ditches and Allah's help, they defeated them.

In this area seven mosques were built, Al–Fateh mosque, Salman Farsi mosque, Ali Ibn Abi Talib mosque, Abu Bakr Siddiq mosque, Umar Ibn Khattab mosque, and Fatima Al-Zahra mosque. There is Masjid Qiblatain nearby which is counted in the seven mosques.

Al-Fateh Mosque

Mosque Fateh or Mosque of Victory is one of the seven mosques at Khandaq. It was built at the top of a hill where the Prophet (SAW) prayed for victory in the the Battle of Khandaq and his prayer was accepted.

He was informed by Jibrael (AS) that his prayers had been accepted and that a strong wind would be sent against the enemy. Surah 33 Ayat 9 to 27 refer to this battle.

Mosque of Salman Al- Farsi

Salman Al- Farsi (RA) was an iranian, who travelled all the way from Iran to Saudi Arabia to learn about Islam. He became one of the close companions of the Prophet (SAW).

The Mosque of Salman Al –Farsi is part of a group of mosques known as the Seven mosques

Garden of Salman Farsi RA

The Prophet (SAW) planted three hundred date palms to free Salman Farsi (RA) from slavery. The date garden of Salman Farsi is near Masjid Quba in Madinah.

Section Three

Some Duas and Prayers

There is no prescribed prayer for Tawaf and Sa'iy. It is best to engage in the remembrance of Allah while performing the Tawaf and Sa'iy. Make any dua or prayer that you remember by heart, but these are just a reminder of some prayers that you can recite with ease.

Kalimas

4 Qul

Darood Sharif, Ibrahimi, Hazara

40 Rabbanas

99 Names of Allah

Tasbih Fatima: Allahu akbar x 34, Alhamdulillah x 33, Subhan Allah x 33

Duas of the Prophets

Ayat Shifa

7 Salaams

Loh-e Quran

Ayat-ul Kursi

Subhanallahi wa bihamdihi

بِسْمِ اللهِ الرَّحْمَنِ الرَّحِيمِ

In the name of Allah, Most Compassionate, Most Merciful

هُوَ اللهُ الَّذِي لَاإِلٰهَ إِلَّا هُوَ

Allah is He besides whom none is worthy of worship

الرَّحْمَنُ	الرَّحِيمُ	الْمَلِكُ	الْقُدُّوسُ	السَّلَامُ
The Compassionate	The Most Merciful	The Sovereign	Free from Blemishes	The Giver of Peace
الْمُؤْمِنُ	الْمُهَيْمِنُ	الْعَزِيزُ	الْجَبَّارُ	الْمُتَكَبِّرُ
Giver of Peace	Giver of Protection	The Mighty	Overpowering Lord	The Self Glorious
الْخَالِقُ	الْبَارِئُ	الْمُصَوِّرُ	الْغَفَّارُ	الْقَهَّارُ
The Creator	The Giver of Life	Fashioner of shapes	Most Forgiving	Almighty Lord
الْوَهَّابُ	الرَّزَّاقُ	الْفَتَّاحُ	الْعَلِيمُ	الْقَابِضُ
Giver of all things	The Sustainer	Remover of Difficulties	The All Knowing	The Straitener
الْبَاسِطُ	الْخَافِضُ	الرَّافِعُ	الْمُعِزُّ	الْمُذِلُّ
Extender of Rizq	One who Humbles	The Exalter	Giver of Honour	Giver of Disgrace
السَّمِيعُ	الْبَصِيرُ	الْحَكَمُ	الْعَدْلُ	اللَّطِيفُ
The All-Hearing	The All-Seeing	The Judge	The Just	Knower of Secrets
الْخَبِيرُ	الْحَلِيمُ	الْعَظِيمُ	الْغَفُورُ	الشَّكُورُ
The Aware	The Clement	The Grand	The All Forgiving	The Grateful
الْعَلِيُّ	الْكَبِيرُ	الْحَفِيظُ	الْمُقِيتُ	الْحَسِيبُ
The High	The Great	The Protector	Controller of things	The Reckoner
الْجَلِيلُ	الْكَرِيمُ	الرَّقِيبُ	الْمُجِيبُ	الْوَاسِعُ
The Majestic	The Benevolent	The Caretaker	Responder to Du'aas	The Ample-Giving

الْحَكِيْمُ The Wise	الْوَدُوْدُ Most Loving	الْمَجِيْدُ Most Venerable	الْبَاعِثُ The Resurrector	الشَّهِيْدُ The Omnipresent	الْحَقُّ The True
الْوَكِيْلُ One in Charge	الْقَوِيُّ The Powerful	الْمَتِيْنُ The Firm	الْوَلِيُّ The Patron	الْحَمِيْدُ The Praiseworthy	الْمُحْصِي The One Who records
الْمُبْدِئُ The Originator	الْمُعِيْدُ One with power to Recreate	الْمُحْيِي Giver of Life	الْمُمِيْتُ Giver of Death	الْحَيُّ Ever living	الْقَيُّوْمُ Self-Subsisting
الْوَاجِدُ The Inventor	الْمَاجِدُ The Excellent	الْوَاحِدُ الْأَحَدُ The One Unequalled		الصَّمَدُ Free from Want	الْقَادِرُ The One with authority
الْمُقْتَدِرُ The One with Full Authority	الْمُقَدِّمُ One Who causes Advancement	الْمُؤَخِّرُ The One Who Retards	الْأَوَّلُ The First	الْآخِرُ The Last	الظَّاهِرُ The Manifest
الْبَاطِنُ The Hidden	الْوَالِي The Authority	الْمُتَعَالِي Above the Creation	الْبَرُّ One who treats with Kindness	التَّوَّابُ The Oft-returning	الْمُنْتَقِمُ The Taker of Retribution
الْعَفُوُّ The Pardoner	الرَّؤُوْفُ The Affectionate	مَالِكُ الْمُلْكِ Possessor of Sovereignty	ذُواالْجَلَالِ وَالْإِكْرَامِ Possessor of Majesty and Benevolence	الْمُقْسِطُ The Just	الْجَامِعُ The Assembler
الْغَنِيُّ Free from Want	الْمُغْنِي The Enricher	الْمُغْطِي The Bestower	الْمَانِعُ The Hinderer	الضَّارُّ The Giver of Distress	النَّافِعُ The Benefactor
النُّوْرُ The Light	الْهَادِي Giver of Guidance	الْبَدِيْعُ The Deviser	الْبَاقِي The Eternal	الْوَارِثُ The Supporter	الرَّشِيْدُ Lover of Virtue

According to the Hadeeth Rasoolullah (S.A.W.) said that there are 99 Beautiful Names of Allah. If anyone makes du'aa through them, his or her du'aa will assuredly be granted. Whoever learns them and recites them will surely enter Jannah. According to another source . . . whoever commits them to memory and recites them constantly will surely enter Jannah.

الصَّبُوْرُ
Most Forbearing

Darood Sharif

Darood-e-Ibrahimi

اَللّٰهُمَّ صَلِّ عَلٰى مُحَمَّدٍ وَّعَلٰى اٰلِ
مُحَمَّدٍ كَمَا صَلَّيْتَ عَلٰى اِبْرَاهِيْمَ وَعَلٰى اٰلِ
اِبْرَاهِيْمَ اِنَّكَ حَمِيْدٌ مَّجِيْدٌ
اَللّٰهُمَّ بَارِكْ عَلٰى مُحَمَّدٍ وَّعَلٰى اٰلِ مُحَمَّدٍ
كَمَا بَارَكْتَ عَلٰى اِبْرَاهِيْمَ وَعَلٰى اٰلِ اِبْرَاهِيْمَ
اِنَّكَ حَمِيْدٌ مَّجِيْدٌ

Darood-e- Hazara

اَللّٰهُمَّ صَلِّ عَلٰى سَيِّدِنَا مُحَمَّدٍ وَّ
عَلٰى اٰلِ سَيِّدِنَا مُحَمَّدٍ بِعَدَدِ كُلِّ ذَرَّةٍ
مِائَةَ اَلْفَ اَلْفَ مَرَّةٍ وَّبَارِكْ وَسَلِّمْ

Easy Darood

اَللّٰهُمَّ صَلِّ عَلٰى سَيِّدِنَا مُحَمَّدٍ
وَعَلٰى اٰلِ سَيِّدِنَا مُحَمَّدٍ
وَبَارِكْ وَسَلِّمْ

O Allah we are sending salutation on the Prophet Mohammad (SAW) and his family, and also sending mercy and blessings.

48

Hadith:

Anas Ibn Mali (RA) narrates that the Prophet (SAW) said: "He who recites a single Darood upon me, Allah blesses him ten times, ten of his sins are forgiven, and he is increased ten times in stages. (Sunan-an-Nasa 1297, Book 13, Hadith 119).

Loh-e Quran

نٓ	حمٓعٓسٓقٓ	الٓمٓٓ
يٰسٓ	حمٓ	الٓمٓصٓ
كهٰيعٓصٓ	قٓ	آمِيٓنَ

Ayatul-Qursi

بِسْمِ اللهِ الرَّحْمٰنِ الرَّحِيْمِ ۝
اللهُ لَا إِلٰهَ إِلَّا هُوَ الْحَيُّ الْقَيُّوْمُ لَا تَأْخُذُهُ سِنَةٌ وَّلَا نَوْمٌ
لَهُ مَا فِى السَّمٰوٰتِ وَمَا فِى الْأَرْضِ مَنْ ذَا الَّذِيْ يَشْفَعُ
عِنْدَهُ إِلَّا بِإِذْنِهِ يَعْلَمُ مَا بَيْنَ أَيْدِيْهِمْ وَمَا خَلْفَهُمْ وَلَا
يُحِيْطُوْنَ بِشَيْءٍ مِّنْ عِلْمِهِ إِلَّا بِمَا شَآءَ وَسِعَ كُرْسِيُّهُ السَّمٰوٰتِ
وَالْأَرْضَ وَلَا يَؤُدُهُ حِفْظُهُمَا وَهُوَ الْعَلِيُّ الْعَظِيْمُ ۝

Dua of Prophet Mohammad (SAW)

رَبَّنَا آتِنَا فِى الدُّنْيَا حَسَنَةً وَّفِى الْآخِرَةِ حَسَنَةً وَّقِنَا عَذَابَ النَّارِ

Translation: "Our Lord, give us in this world that which is good and in the hereafter that which is good and protect us from the punishment of the fire."

Surah Fateha

Surah Ikhlas

Dua for beneficial knowledge, provision and accepted deeds

اَللّٰهُمَّ إِنِّي أَسْأَلُكَ عِلْمًا نَافِعًا،

وَرِزْقًا طَيِّبًا، وَعَمَلًا مُّتَقَبَّلًا،

Translation: O Allah, I ask You for beneficial knowledge, goodly provision and acceptable deeds (Sunan Ibn Majah: 925).

Dua for protection from all evil

بِسْمِ اللهِ الَّذِىْ لَا يَضُرُّ مَعَ اسْمِهٖ شَىْءٌ فِى الْاَرْضِ
وَلَا فِى السَّمَآءِ وَهُوَ السَّمِيْعُ الْعَلِيْمُ

Translation: In the name of Allah with whose name there is protection against every kind of harm in the earth or in the heaven, and He is the All-Hearing and All-Knowing. (Abu Dawood & Al-Tirmidhi).

Dua of Prophet Adam (AS)

This is the dua Prophet Adam (AS) made for forgiveness when he was sent out of heaven to Earth.

رَبَّنَا ظَلَمْنَا أَنفُسَنَا وَإِن لَّمْ تَغْفِرْ لَنَا وَتَرْحَمْنَا لَنَكُونَنَّ مِنَ الْخَاسِرِينَ

Translation: Our Lord, we have wronged ourselves, and if You do not forgive us and have mercy upon us, we will surely be among the losers. (Quran: Surah Al-Araf 7:23)

Dua of Prophet Yunus (AS)

This is the dua Prophet Yunus (AS) made when he was swallowed by a whale.

لَّا إِلَٰهَ إِلَّا أَنتَ سُبْحَٰنَكَ إِنِّى كُنتُ مِنَ الظَّٰلِمِينَ ۞

Translation: There is no God except You; exalted are You, Indeed, I have been of the wrongdoers. Quran 21:87.

Bibliography

- Hajj and Umrah according to Sunnah, by Maulana Mukhtar Ahmed Nadvi, Saheeh International

- Messages for Pilgrims and those Performing Umrah, by Dr. Yahya bin Ibraaheem Al-Yahya, World Organisation Presenting Islam

- How to Perform Ziyarah by Shaykh Muhammad Saleem Dhorat, Islamic Da'wah Academy

- Madinah Monawwarah Sites to Visit 1440

- How to Perform Umrah by Shaykh Muhammad Saleem Dhorat

- Umrah Guide, Al-Hidaayah Travel

- Wikipedia

- Islamic Landmarks.com

- The Holy Quran

Other books in this series

1. Umrah Made Easy
A concise book on Umrah to carry with you as perform Umrah.

2. Ziyarahs
A concise book on visiting the Ziyarahs in Makkah and Madinah.

3. Ayesha Goes for Umrah
This book is a coloured picture book to guide children going for Umrah.

Other books by Dr. Farah Alam- Mirza

Islamic Education for Children Series

4. Islamic Manners for Children

5. Who is Allah?

6. What is Eid-ul Adha?

7. Let's go to the Masjid

Healthy Kids Series

8. Wash Your Hands

9. Ouch, I Need a Plaster!

10. Drink Up

11. An Itchy Round Rash

12. Achoo! Catch it! Bin it! Kill it!

13. 5-a-Day Every Day

14. Brush Your Teeth

15. Sunkissed

16. Crystal Clear!

17. No More Nits!

And more to come…

Medical Book

18. 1500 Questions for the MRCPCH/ DCH, Foundation of Practice Exam

Biographies

19. M. Yamin Qureshi- Celebration of a Decorated Life

20. Shahida Parvin Alam- Anthology of a Beautiful Life

Printed in Great Britain
by Amazon